Baltimore Bouquets

by Mimi Dietrich

Patterns and Techniques for Dimensional Appliqué

Dedication

To my students and friends who have shared the Baltimore Appliqué dream. You have felt the magic of the history, been brave enough to take those first stitches, and created albums of very special memories.

Acknowledgments

Baltimore Bouquets started with a quilting class at Seminole Sampler in Catonsville, Maryland. Markie Lawrence and Kaye Pelovitz talked me into teaching a year-long Baltimore Album quilt class, and a wonderful adventure began. Many thanks to Markie and Kaye for providing a place for everything to happen.

We were all inspired by Jeana Kimball and Elly Sienkiewicz. Their Baltimore Album patterns provided the basis for all of our quilts, and their writings gave us a new appreciation for our hometown history.

Carol Watson signed up as a student in the class and delighted everyone with her creative approaches to the designs. Thanks to Carol for sharing her Thistle and Sweet Pea designs.

Edith Tanniru of American Beauty Fabrics (610 Hamilton Parkway, DeWitt, New York 13214) excited us all with her Baltimore Crush fabric medley and provided hand-dyed fabrics for the American Beauty Antique quilt.

When I first started to dream about this book, Marion Shelton said, "You can do it"; Bob Dietrich said, "Sure, you can do it." My students stitched the designs for the quilts. Then, Nancy Martin and her staff at That Patchwork Place made this all come true. Many thanks to all of you!

Credits

Editor	Ann Price
Copy Editor	Liz McGehee
Cover Design	Judy Petry
Text Design	Connie Lunde
Illustrations and Graphics	Stephanie Benson
	Linda Campbell
Photography	Brian Kaplan

Baltimore Bouquets©
©1992 by Mimi Dietrich

That Patchwork Place, Inc., PO Box 118, Bothell, WA 98041-0118

Printed in Hong Kong
02 01 00 99   12 11 10

Library of Congress Cataloging–in–Publication Data
Dietrich, Mimi.
    Baltimore bouquets / by Mimi Dietrich; [illustration and graphics, Stephanie Benson, Linda Campbell].
        p.   cm.
    ISBN 1-56477-010-9:
        1. Appliqué—Patterns.   2. Album quilts—Maryland—Baltimore.
3. Patchwork—Patterns.   I. Title.
TT779.D54   1992
746.9'7—dc20
                                            92-10358
                                            CIP

Contents

Introduction

I live just outside the city limits of Baltimore, Maryland. I grew up here. I have many fond memories of family rides to the city to visit the B & O train museum, the Washington Monument, and the white marble steps of the Baltimore row houses. I've traveled to Oregon and Vermont, to Mississippi and Texas, but I always come home to Baltimore. My quilting has somewhat the same story. I've made an Ohio Star and a Lone Star and used up many rotary cutter blades making pieced quilts, but I really love to stitch appliqué quilts.

One of my most memorable trips to the city was in 1981. I went with a group of quilting friends to see an exhibit of antique Baltimore Album quilts at the Baltimore Museum of Art. The intricate designs seemed impossible and the stitches were incredibly tiny. But the beauty of the colors and patterns was unforgettable. About this time, I had the great fortune to meet Elsie Spencer, a wonderful quilter who taught appliqué based on patterns from antique album quilts. My hometown love for appliqué quilts was inevitable!

In 1984 I shared an adventure in appliqué with eight friends. We met for a year and exchanged small Baltimore-style blocks. We stitched the same block each month so that we would all have the same designs, but the block arrangements and different border designs have made each quilt special.

In 1990 the Baltimore Heritage Quilters' Guild made a full-sized album quilt under the leadership of Robert Wilson. What seemed an impossible task became a reality as forty members of the group appliquéd and quilted, recreating history in Baltimore. This experience prompted many members to begin album quilts of their own.

My latest project has been teaching a year-long class on Baltimore Album quilts. Seventy-five students met in five groups once a month to share ideas, inspire each other, and increase their skill, using a variety of appliqué methods. It has been a delight to watch my students recreate traditional designs, originate their own interpretations, and stitch memories into their quilts. Some of their favorite techniques included creating dimensional flowers. They folded and gathered fabric into buds and blossoms, producing flowers that bloomed creatively in many quilt blocks.

In **Baltimore Bouquets** I have adapted these techniques to create twenty small appliqué blocks based on the Baltimore designs. The blocks can be arranged in many combinations with four borders. My students have eagerly stitched the blocks for the quilts. I hope they will inspire you to start a small quilt or wall hanging of your own. We send our "Bouquets from Baltimore" to you!

Mimi Dietrich

Fabrics and Supplies

Suggested Fabrics

When choosing fabric for appliqué, you need fabric for two purposes: the background fabric and the appliqué pieces.

Background fabrics are usually solid, light colors or small prints that complement the appliqué design. White background fabrics add brightness and clarity to pastel appliqués. Off-white backgrounds enhance the richness of darker appliqué palettes. White-on-white or white-on-muslin prints make lovely backgrounds for stitchers who like a subtle print rather than a solid-colored fabric. A fabulous "tea-dyed" print gives an antique glow to a quilt. Appliqués stitched on a dark background create a wonderfully dramatic effect.

Fabrics used for the appliqué pieces should be appropriate for the design. Consider the proper color and print size for the pattern you are stitching.

Traditionally, Baltimore Album quilts are made with a palette of dark red and green fabrics, adding touches of blue, pink, brown, and yellow. This is always appropriate, but it's also fun to create the designs in soft pastels. Brighter folk-art colors, with deep blues and golds added to the reds and greens, will also change the appearance of your quilt. If blue is your favorite color, try using only shades of blue. If you have a favorite multicolored print, use the print for the border, then select appliqué fabrics that coordinate with the colors in the print.

To preview the fabrics you choose, cut the shape of your appliqué piece as a "window" in a piece of paper. Place the window over your fabric to view the effect.

Solid-colored fabrics are always "safe" to use, but printed fabrics can make your designs more exciting. Fabric printed in shades of one color can be very effective for representing features in flowers and leaves. The tone-on-tone fabrics (for example, dark green printed over light green) have a solid-colored effect with a subtle texture. Sometimes, the design printed on the fabric creates lines that can become veins in leaves, or textures in flower petals.

Fabrics printed with actual flowers and leaves are fun to use. Cut out whole flowers or individual petals and leaves to give a realistic effect to your appliqués.

Use a basket-weave print for baskets or a wood-grain print for stems.

Use several shades or values of the same color to add realism to flowers. Fabrics printed by the same manufacturer may be available in different prints with similar colors. Hand-dyed fabrics available in light to dark gradations are wonderful for shading flowers and leaves.

Tie-dyed fabrics are fun to use because the light and dark areas of the fabric blend well together. A leaf can be cut so that two tones are positioned on either side of the center to create a vein. If you use a shaded fabric for flower petals, position the darker area of the fabric in the center of the flower.

Be brave and try using the right and wrong sides of the same fabric to shade flowers, ribbons, and bows. It may seem strange to use the wrong side, but it often has a wonderful effect.

Large-scale prints may seem inappropriate for appliqué, but cut a small piece from a specific area and you may have the perfect flower petals or bird wings. Use the "window" to help you decide.

Create balance in your quilt by repeating fabrics in several of the designs. Repeat the same flower, or duplicate a flower fabric in a bud. If you are using four blocks in your quilt, balance colors and shapes in opposite diagonal designs.

Border fabrics are important because they provide a framework for your designs. Use a multicolored print for your border swags, then choose colors from the print to build your color scheme for the quilt. Use darker fabrics in the borders to add a frame to your work and accent the colors within the designs.

If you have enough appliqué fabric, make a color "paste-up" of your colors before you start to stitch. Trace your pattern onto a sheet of paper, cut fabric shapes, and glue them to the design. This will give you a good idea of the color arrangement as you make your decisions before stitching. Use this paste-up as a placement guide for the fabrics as you stitch.

Cotton fabrics are easy to handle for appliqué. Synthetic fabrics tend to fray more than cotton and are often slippery. Sometimes, however, a favorite fabric contains synthetic fibers, and it's worth a little extra care to use it in your design.

Prewash all fabrics to prevent shrinking and bleeding in your quilt. Wash dark and light colors separately so that the dark colors do not run onto the light colors. Make sure the dark colors are washed and rinsed (several times, if necessary) so they will not bleed onto light background fabrics. To test, cut a small piece of appliqué fabric. Wet this piece and place it on a scrap of background fabric to test for colorfastness. If color shows up on the background scrap, you need to wash your fabric again, or perhaps choose a different fabric. Press the fabrics smooth so the pieces will be accurate when they are cut out.

Supplies

Needles

Size is the most important consideration in choosing a needle for appliqué. A fine needle will glide easily through the edges of the appliqué pieces, creating small stitches and helping the thread blend into the fabrics. Size 10 (fine) to size 12 (very fine) sharp needles work well. Try different types of needles and you will soon find the one most comfortable for you. If a fine needle is difficult to thread, use a needle threader to insert the thread through the needle eye.

Thread

Thread used for appliqué should match the color of the appliqué pieces rather than the background fabric. If it is not possible to match the color exactly, choose thread that is a little darker than the fabric.

Gray thread will often blend in when the perfect color cannot be found.

All-cotton thread works well for stitching appliqués. It is pliable and blends invisibly into the edges of the appliqués. If cotton thread is not available in just the right color, use cotton-covered polyester thread.

Pins

Small straight pins are used to pin-baste the appliqué pieces to the background fabric. Fine ¾" sequin pins work well because they don't catch the threads as you sew.

Scissors

Small embroidery scissors are ideal for trimming appliqué pieces. Sharp blades that cut to the point are necessary for clipping inner points on some appliqué pieces.

Marking Pencils

Several markers can be used to trace the pattern designs onto the background fabric. On light fabrics, I like to use a silver marking pencil, available from most quilt shops. You can also use a regular pencil (#2 or #3) or a fine-lead (.5 mm) mechanical pencil. A chalk marker shows up well on dark fabrics. Whichever marking tool you use, test it on a sample of your fabric before using it on your quilt. Make sure you can see the lines and that they can be removed.

Yardage Requirements

Use the following yardage requirements as a general guideline when planning your quilt and purchasing fabrics.

Yardage Requirements: 44"-wide fabric

Background fabric:
   30" quilt (4 designs): 1⅜ yds.
   40" quilt (9 designs): 1¾ yds.

Cut 4 borders, each 5½" wide, across the width of your fabric. Use the remaining fabric to cut the 12½"-square blocks.

Appliqué fabric:
   Small pieces (¼ yd.) of appropriate colors:
      3 shades of red (or predominant
         flower color)
      3 shades of green (or predominant
         leaf color)
      blue, pink, purple, yellow, gold, brown

Narrow border and binding: ½ yd.

Backing fabric: (usually the same as background)
   30" quilt: 1 yd.
   40" quilt: 1¼ yds.

Appliqué Methods

There are many techniques for preparing appliqué pieces. Some stitchers use traditional methods, marking the fabrics with a pencil and basting the seam allowances. Others use needle-turn methods to form the shapes as they stitch. If you have a favorite method, use it to enjoy stitching the designs.

Freezer-Paper Method

I like to use freezer paper to make precise pattern pieces. These templates help create perfectly shaped appliqués because the paper sticks to the fabric and controls the shape. This method also helps improve accuracy in repeated designs, such as the border swags.

1. Place the freezer paper, plastic side down, on your pattern. Trace each appliqué design with a sharp pencil. For this technique, pattern pieces
   Freezer paper
   with asymmetrical shapes (for example, the partial leaves, bird, bow, sweet peas, and cornucopia) must be traced in reverse. Trace the shape on clear template plastic, flip the plastic over, then trace the reversed design onto the freezer paper.

2. Cut out the freezer-paper shapes on the pencil line. Do not add seam allowances.

3. Place the plastic side of the freezer-paper against the wrong side of the appliqué fabric. Iron the freezer-paper shape to the wrong side of the fabric, using a dry, hot iron.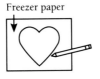
   Wrong side of fabric

4. Cut out the fabric shape, adding a ¼"-wide seam allowance.

5. Fold the seam allowance snugly over the freezer paper to form the appliqué shape, except on edges that will lie flat under other appliqué pieces. Hand baste seam allowances down, stitching through the paper.

6. Pin the shape to the background fabric, using ¾" sequin pins.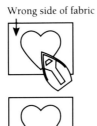

7. Appliqué the shape onto the background fabric.

8. Remove any basting stitches. If there is an opening in the appliqué, remove the freezer paper with a small pair of tweezers. If the appliqué is completely stitched, cut a small slit in the background fabric behind the appliqué and remove the freezer paper.

9. Press the completed appliqué from the wrong side.

Traditional Appliqué Stitch

The traditional appliqué stitch is appropriate for sewing all areas of appliqué designs. It works well on straight areas as well as sharp points and curves. It can also be used to tack down fabric pieces for dimensional techniques.

Start with a single strand of thread about 18" long. Tie a knot in one end. To hide your knot, slip your needle into the seam allowance from the wrong side of the appliqué piece, bringing it out along the fold line. The knot will be hidden inside the seam allowance.

Take the first stitch by moving your needle straight off the appliqué and inserting it into the background fabric. If you are right-handed, stitch from right to left. If you are left-handed, stitch from left to right.

Guide the needle under the background fabric parallel to the edge of the appliqué, bringing it up about ⅛" away, along the pattern line.

As you bring the needle back up, catch only one or two threads of the folded edge of the appliqué piece. Take the next stitch by moving the needle straight off the appliqué edge and inserting it into the background fabric. Again, guide the needle under the background, bringing it up about ⅛" away and catching the edge of the appliqué. Give the thread a slight tug and continue stitching.

From the right side, the only visible parts of the stitch are small dots of thread along the appliqué edge. On the wrong side, you'll see stitches ⅛" long. The stitch length should be consistent, though smaller stitches are sometimes necessary for curves and points.

When you get to the end of your stitching, pull your needle through to the wrong side. Take two small stitches behind the appliqué piece, making knots by bringing your needle through the loops. Before you cut your thread, take a moment to see if the thread will be shadowing through your background when you finish. If you think it will, take one more small stitch behind the appliqué to direct the tail of the thread under the appliqué fabric, then clip the thread.

Dimensional Techniques

Add texture and variety to your appliqué patterns as you learn to use the dimensional techniques in this chapter. Fold, gather, or stuff your appliqué fabrics and enjoy new creative effects.

Stems

⅛" Stems

Cut fabric into ½"-wide bias strips. These can be cut easily with a rotary cutter, using a clear acrylic ruler as a cutting guide.

Cut these strips into pieces ½" longer than the stem design on the pattern. This allows for a ¼"-wide seam allowance at each end to be covered by leaves or flowers.

Fold the strips in half lengthwise, wrong sides together, and press with a steam iron.

Place a folded strip on a stem design that has been drawn onto the background fabric, so the raw edges touch one line of the stem and the folded edge extends past the other line.

Using small running stitches, sew the strip to the background fabric through the center of the strip, slightly toward the raw edge. Sew a backstitch every few stitches to secure the stem. This line of stitching should match the covered stem line.

Roll the folded edge over the seam allowance. Appliqué the fold to the background fabric to create a smooth, thin stem.

¼" Stems

Cut fabric into ½"-wide bias strips.

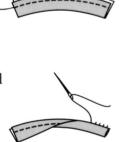

Fold one long edge, wrong sides together, turning in ⅛". Baste along the fold, using small running stitches. Then, fold and baste the other long edge so the raw edges meet in the middle of the strip. This results in a neat ¼"-wide strip that can be applied straight or on a curve. Cut the length you need plus ¼" at each end to layer under other appliqué pieces.

Stuffed Stems

Stems can be stuffed to create a realistic effect. Use a single strand of knitting yarn and a blunt tapestry needle to thread the yarn through the appliquéd stem. Trim the yarn at the seam line to avoid bulk under other appliqués.

Leaves

Full Leaves

Baste under the seam allowance around the entire leaf. To create sharp points at the ends of the leaves, first fold the point of the fabric in toward the appliqué. Next, fold the right side under, then the left, to form the sharp point.

As you appliqué the point of the leaf, take your last stitch on the first side very close to the point. Take the next stitch on the second side of the point. A stitch on each side, close to the point, will accent the outside point. Do not put a stitch directly on the point, as it tends to flatten the point.

If the full leaf is positioned next to a stem, start to appliqué the leaf ¼" before it touches the stem. Take one or two appliqué stitches between the leaf and the stem to connect them.

Stitch around the entire leaf shape. To remove the freezer paper, cut a small slit in the background fabric behind the appliqué and use tweezers to pull out the paper.

Partial Leaves

When a leaf is positioned under a flower or another leaf, it creates a partial leaf shape. The leaf seam allowance is not turned under in the covered area. Baste under the seam allowances on edges that will be appliquéd. Stitch the leaf edges to the background fabric, leaving the covered seam allowance open. Pull the freezer paper out through the open edge. If the opening is large, baste the seam allowance to the background to keep it flat under the flower or leaf.

Pinched Leaves

As an alternate method for stitching partial leaves, add a pinch to the leaf to make it dimensional.

Make a freezer-paper pattern of the leaf shape. Cut a slit from the center of the open edge to the point, stopping before you get to the tip. Iron the freezer paper to the leaf fabric, spreading the base of the leaf apart ¼". Cut out the fabric leaf with this extra fullness. Pinch the excess fabric in the center of the leaf to bring the paper edges back together. Appliqué the leaf edges to the shape lines on the background fabric. Remove the paper, then baste across the seam allowance to secure the pinched fabric.

Clip

1/4"

For another effect, gather the base of the leaf with small stitches instead of pinching.

Lined Leaves

Lined leaves create another alternative for partial leaf shapes. Cut out a freezer-paper leaf shape and iron it to the wrong side of your leaf fabric. Place this fabric right sides together with another piece of leaf fabric. Cut out the leaf shape, adding a ¼"-wide seam allowance. Using small stitches, machine stitch around the outside edges of the freezer paper, leaving an opening where the leaf will be covered by a flower. Trim the stitched seam allowance to ⅛". Remove the freezer paper, turn the leaf right side out, and press. Baste the open seam allowance in place on the background fabric. When you appliqué the covering flower, make sure your stitches go through to the background to secure the leaf. Let the leaf shape remain unattached. Use two shades of fabric for your leaves (darker underneath) to add to the dimensional effect.

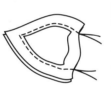

Buds

Folded Buds

To make a folded bud, cut a 1¼" square of fabric. Fold the square diagonally, wrong sides together.

Fold each side point down to the center point, overlapping the points so they are about ¼" from

the bottom point. Baste along the bottom edges of the bud.

If necessary, trim the raw edges of the bud so that it will fit within the markings for the calyx (base of the bud). Baste the bud within the calyx seam allowance. Let the bud remain free, or appliqué the outside edges of the bud, leaving the folds unstitched. Appliqué the calyx over the raw edges of the bud.

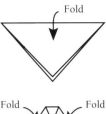

Fold

Fold   Fold

Gathered Buds

Cut a 2"-diameter circle of fabric. Sew a small running stitch around the outside edge of the circle.

Gather the edge of the circle together, keeping the right side of the fabric out. Form the bud, pulling all of the gathers in one direction.

Adjust the gathers so that the bud fits within the markings for the calyx. Tie a knot in the gathering threads.

Appliqué the outside edges of the bud. Appliqué the calyx over the raw edges of the bud.

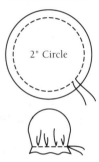

2" Circle

Posies

Freezer paper will help keep the petals of your flowers neat and consistent. Carefully clip the seam allowance between the petals. Clip within two or three threads to eliminate "fuzzies" between the petals.

As you appliqué at the inner points, use the tip of the needle with a dab of glue from a glue stick to push under the threads. Take smaller stitches within ¼" of the point. Stitch past the point, then return to add one extra stitch for emphasis. Come up through the appliqué at the point, catching a little more fabric—four or five threads instead of one or two. Make a straight stitch outward, inserting the needle under the appliqué. Pull the thread slightly to accentuate the point.

A few close stitches will tack the fabric securely and keep the inner points from fraying. If your thread matches your appliqué fabric, these stitches will blend in with the edge of the shape.

Clip

Freezer Paper

Roses

Layered Roses

A layered rose is composed of four appliqué pieces: a large base piece, two paisley-shaped petals, and a small center. The base piece will determine the basic color of your rose. The paisley petals should be the same color as the base but should be lighter or darker so that they do not disappear into the background. Each petal can be different, or the two can be made from the same fabric. The center piece is small but adds depth to the rose. It should be darker than the other fabrics. In some of the antique Baltimore Album quilts, a small flower from a calico was positioned in the rose center. White roses appeared frequently in these quilts, and it's fun to recreate them, using today's fabrics.

To appliqué the layered rose, begin with the base piece. Then, appliqué the small center to the base, turning under the top curve. Leave the rest of the seam allowance free to be covered by the paisley petals. Appliqué the two petals to complete the rose. One petal slightly overlaps the other.

For added texture, embroider a few French knots in the center of the rose.

Stuffed Roses

Appliqué the base piece for the rose. Stuff the base lightly by fluffing a small amount of fiberfill and spreading it within the shape. Add the stuffing before you finish the appliqué, or cut a small slit in the background fabric behind the appliqué to add the stuffing. As you appliqué the rose center and petals, stitch through all layers to add puffiness to the rose. For more dimension, add extra stuffing to the petals.

Yoyo Flowers

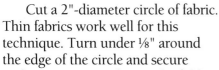

Cut a 2"-diameter circle of fabric. Thin fabrics work well for this technique. Turn under ⅛" around the edge of the circle and secure with a running stitch near the fold. Cut a circle of heavy paper the size of the finished flower and place the paper in the center of the fabric. Gather the edges together in the center of the circle and

press to create smooth edges. Remove the paper and tie a secure knot. If the fabric edges do not meet tightly, take a few stitches back and forth to close the hole. These stitches can be covered with French knots later.

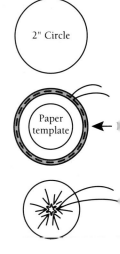

Insert the needle straight down through the center of the gathers, bringing it through to the wrong side to tie a knot. Appliqué the edges of the circle to the background fabric. Add a few French knots or beads to accent the center of the flower.

Gathered Blossoms

Cut a 2¼"-diameter circle of fabric. Thin fabrics work well for this technique. Turn under ⅛" around the edge of the circle and secure with a running stitch near the fold. Gather the edges together in the center of the circle and tie a secure knot. If the edges do not meet tightly, take a few stitches back and forth to close the hole. Insert the needle straight down through the center of the gathers, bringing it through to the back side.

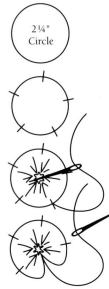

With the gathered side up, divide the edges of the flower into five equal petals as shown, marking lightly with a fabric marker. To make the petals, bring the thread from the back over the outside edge of the flower and insert it into the center again. Place the thread at one of the edge markings, then pull the thread to create a petal. Continue looping the thread over the edges to create five petals. Knot the thread on the back of the flower, then tack the flower to the background fabric. Add French knots or beads to the center.

Gathered Flowers

Gathered flowers add a special touch to Baltimore appliqué designs. Using a technique known as "ruching," you can create textured roses with red fabric or vibrant chrysanthemums with warm, rich autumn colors.

Use a rotary cutter and ruler to cut a straight-grain strip of fabric 1⅛" wide x 25" long.

With wrong sides together, fold and baste ¼" along one long edge. Then, fold and baste the other long edge, having the raw edges meet in the middle of the strip.

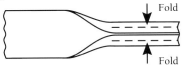

For an alternate method of making the fabric strip, cut a strip 1⅝" wide x 25" long. Fold the strip right sides together and sew a ¼" seam, using small stitches on your sewing machine. Trim the seam to a scant ⅛", then turn the strip right side out. Press the strip flat, with the seam in the center back of the strip.

Lay your strip right side up on the guide at the bottom of the page. Use a fabric marker to place dots on the folded edges of your strip at 1" intervals. Mark the entire length of the strip.

Stitch a zigzag gathering stitch. Starting at one end of the strip, bring your needle out through the bottom folded edge, then take two or three small stitches on the fold to lock the thread. Stitch from dot to dot, taking a stitch over the folded edge when you change direction.

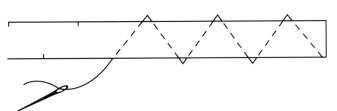

Stitch about 8" before pulling the thread to gather the fabric. Pull the thread in a straight line, gathering fabric petals on each side. Pull the thread tight, then adjust the fabric to spread the petals slightly. Continue stitching until you have 21 petals on each edge.

Use a second needle and thread to form the flower. To begin, trim the beginning edge to ¼", then turn this seam allowance under the first petal and tack it securely. Arrange the first five petals into a circle, then take a stitch in the first five "inside" petals to draw them together.

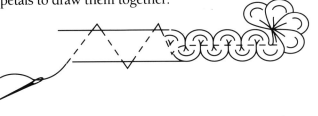

Carefully arrange the sixth petal slightly under the first one to begin making a second row of petals. Turn the flower to the wrong side and tack the inside petals to the back (¼" inside the edge) as you form the flower.

When you get to the end of the flower, taper the last petal under the first row, adjusting it to form a smooth shape. You may need to add a few petals. As you finish, your gathering stitches should stop on the outside edge of the strip. Pull the thread to make the last petal and knot the thread. Cut the strip ¼" beyond the last stitch, then slip the raw edges under the previous row.

After the flower is formed, start at the outside edge and appliqué the petals securely to the background fabric. Stitch the center edge of each petal and each inner point. Your stitches will move in a spiral toward the center of the flower.

Add a few French knots or beads to the center of the flower to accent the color.

Bluebells

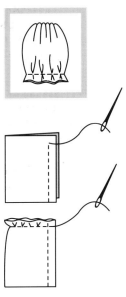

Cut a rectangle of blue fabric 2" x 1½". Fold the rectangle in half, right sides together, to measure 1" x 1½". Sew a ¼"-wide seam, using small running stitches. Tie a knot at the top of the seam but do *not* cut the thread. Using the same thread and small running stitches, stitch around the top, ¼" from the edge. Pull the thread to gather the top of the bluebell, then tie a secure knot. Carefully turn the bluebell right side out. Fold up a generous ¼" at the bottom edge to form a hem. Arrange the bluebell so that the side seam is at the back of the bluebell. Stitching through all layers, sew a running stitch across the bottom of the bluebell ¼" from the bottom edge. Pull the stitches gently to give the flower its shape. Tie a knot in the thread to secure the shape. Appliqué the bluebell, sewing the back layer of the flower to the background fabric.

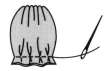

Actual-size guide for gathered flower

Circles

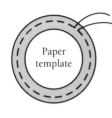

Cut a template of heavy paper, such as a manila folder, the exact size of the finished circle. Cut fabric circles, adding a ¼"-wide seam allowance around the edge of the template. Sew a small running stitch around the fabric circle. Keep the stitches within the seam allowance, not too close to the edge. Place the paper template in the center of the fabric circle. Pull the thread ends to make a crisp circle. Steam press the circle, then let it rest a minute. Carefully peel back the fabric and remove the paper. Gently pull the basting threads to tighten the seam allowance and make it lie flat. Tie a knot and trim the threads. Pin the circle to the background fabric and appliqué with smaller-than-usual stitches.

Ribbons and Bows

Bows with three loops were often stitched into the appliqué patterns in the traditional Baltimore Album quilts. The bows are stitched in six separate pieces. A dimensional effect can be created by using two shades of the same color, or possibly the right and wrong sides of the same fabric. Appliqué the right streamer first, then the side loops, then the left streamer and center loop. Cover the raw edges in the center with a circle.

The ribbons tied at the bottom of many wreaths are stitched in three parts. Appliqué the two streamers first, extending the seam allowance into the center circle. Cover the raw edges by stitching a circle in the center.

The two streamers can be lined (like Lined Leaves, page 9) and remain unattached.

Embroidery Stitches

Stem Stitch

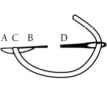

The stem stitch is used to stitch thin flower stems. Using two strands of embroidery floss in your needle, bring the needle up through the fabric at point A. Insert the needle at B, about ¼" away, and come up again at C, halfway between A and B. Pull the thread through, holding the thread below the needle.

To continue the stitch, insert the needle at D and come up again at B, the same place where the needle went into the fabric for the last stitch. Pull the thread through, always holding the thread below the needle.

Continue by repeating the stitches. Each stitch will touch the previous one, creating a smooth line.

French Knots

French knots are used for flower centers and to create baby's breath in the baskets and bouquets.

Using two strands of embroidery floss in your needle, bring the needle up through the fabric at point A. Wind the thread around the needle twice as shown.

Carefully insert the needle into the fabric right next to point A. Gently tug the thread so that the twists on the needle lie at the base of the needle.

Slowly pull the needle down through the fabric to create a perfect French knot.

To create larger French knots, use three or four strands of floss.

Patterns

How to Use the Patterns

The patterns in this book are printed full size. In all of the quilts, the finished size of the blocks is 10" square. The background fabric blocks are cut 10½" square to include seam allowances. Because appliqué blocks often become distorted or frayed during stitching, I like to cut the squares 1" larger all around (12½"), then trim them neatly to the correct size after I've completed the appliqué.

To place the appliqué pieces onto the background fabric accurately, mark the design on the fabric. If your background fabric is white or off-white, simply trace the design onto your fabric.

If you cannot see through your background fabric, use a light box. If you do not have one, you can create your own by separating your dining-room table as if adding an extra leaf. Place a storm window or other piece of glass, plastic, or Plexiglas over the opening. Set a table lamp on the floor underneath the glass and you have an instant light table. Place your pattern on the glass, then your fabric on top of the pattern. The light will shine through so you can easily trace your design.

To trace the patterns, fold your background fabric square into quarters. Place the folds on the vertical and horizontal center lines marked on each pattern, matching the center of the design. Trace the pattern design onto the background fabric, using a washable fabric marker. Test the marker on a scrap of background fabric before marking your quilt.

To make templates for appliqué, trace the appliqué patterns onto freezer paper. Place the freezer paper, plastic side down, on your pattern. Trace the design with a sharp pencil. Patterns for asymmetrical shapes (for example, the partial leaves, bird, bow, sweet peas, and cornucopia) must be traced in reverse. Trace the shape onto clear template plastic, flip the plastic over, then trace the reversed design onto the freezer paper.

Cut out the freezer-paper templates and iron them to the wrong side of the appliqué fabric. Cut out the fabric shapes, adding ¼"-wide seam allowances around the outside of the freezer paper.

Some leaves are complete shapes. Other leaves are partial and should be cut out in the shape that you see. (Do not add lines to make full leaves.) Partial leaves are usually positioned under other leaves or flowers. Stitch these first, letting the seam allowance lie flat where it will be covered. Most flowers are cut from freezer paper exactly as they are pictured. Stems, yoyo flowers, gathered blossoms, and gathered flowers are not cut from freezer paper but are cut from strips of fabric or circles, which are described in the directions for "Dimensional Techniques," beginning on page 8.

You'll find directions for stitching the designs with each pattern. A recommended stitching sequence is given, as well as directions for techniques not covered in "Dimensional Techniques."

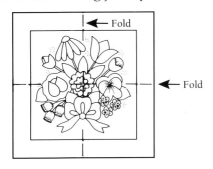

Flower Bouquet

1. Trace the design onto your background fabric.

2. Referring to "Appliqué Methods" (page 7) and "Dimensional Techniques" (page 8), stitch the pieces in the following order:
   - ⅛" stems
   - leaves (except the lower left leaf)
   - folded bud
   - gathered bud
   - layered rose
   - lower left leaf that overlaps the rose
   - gathered blossoms
   - gathered flower
   - bluebells
   - bow

3. The pansy is stitched in three pieces. Appliqué the top petals first, overlap the center petals, then add the bottom petals. Add a few straight stitches with embroidery floss to bring the pansy to life.

4. The black-eyed Susan is the state flower of Maryland and is proper in any Baltimore Bouquet. Appliqué each petal separately, leaving the top seam allowance open. A small bit of fiberfill may be stuffed into each petal. Cover the seam allowances as you add the top of the flower. Embroider a few French knots for a realistic look.

5. Appliqué the tulip in three pieces, beginning with the center petal. Add the two outer petals, stitching them together at the bottom.

6. Embroider the bluebell stems with the stem stitch, then stitch the French knots to add baby's breath to your bouquet.

Flower Bouquet

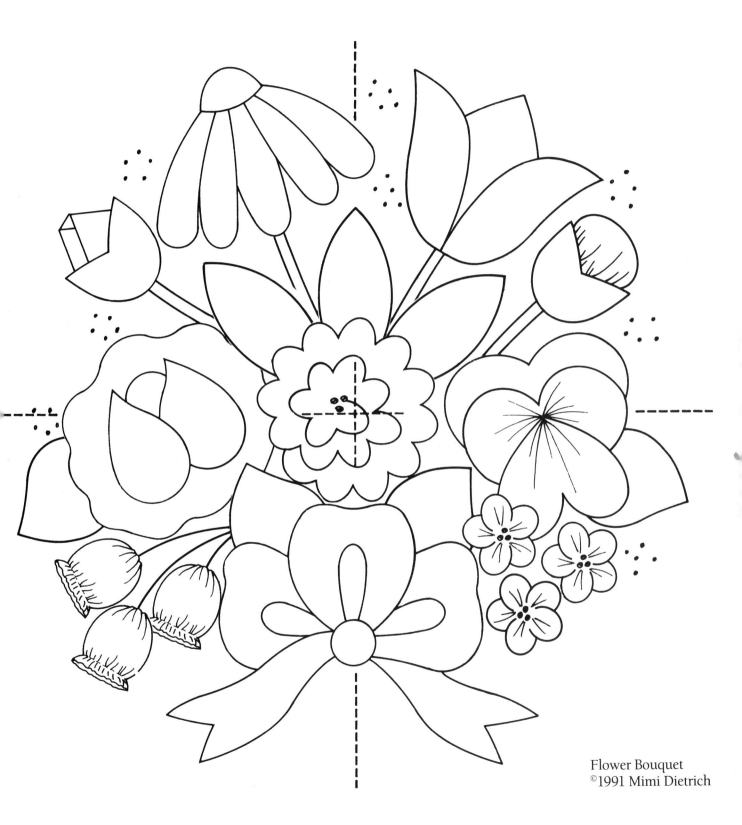

Flower Bouquet
©1991 Mimi Dietrich

Rose Bouquet

1. Trace the design onto your background fabric.
2. Referring to "Appliqué Methods" (page 7) and "Dimensional Techniques" (page 8), stitch the pieces in the following order:

    ⅛" stems
    three center leaves
    folded buds
    layered roses
    two lower leaves
    bow
3. Embroider the French knots to add baby's breath to your bouquet.

Rose Bouquet

Rose Bouquet
©1991 Mimi Dietrich

Album Basket

1. Trace the design onto your background fabric.

2. Referring to "Appliqué Methods" (page 7) and "Dimensional Techniques" (page 8), stitch the pieces in the following order:

⅛" stem	posy
leaves	layered rose
folded bud	gathered blossom
gathered bud	bluebells

3. Appliqué the bird in three separate pieces. Appliqué the left wing first, then the body, then the right wing. Add a French knot or a bead for the bird's eye. For fun, stuff the wings lightly or line them and keep them unattached. Choose fabrics to simulate the texture of the bird's feathers.

4. Cut ½"-wide bias strips of basket fabric. Baste the strips to make ¼" stems, then cut the strips ½" longer than the basket lines in the pattern. Appliqué the vertical basket lines first, leaving the left and right sides unstitched where the top edges go under (where asterisks are located in drawing). Appliqué the top of the basket, tucking the ends under the sides. Finish stitching the vertical lines. Appliqué the basket base to complete the basket.

Leave unstitched between marks.

The top edge of the basket can be braided, using three ¼"-wide stems cut 12" long. Pin the three strip ends together, then braid the strips, always keeping the seam allowances of the strips next to the background fabric. Pin the braid to the basket top and cut the braid ¼" longer at each end. Turn under the ends and appliqué the edges of the braid to the basket top.

5. An open album can be made, using a lined front cover, a back cover, and an inside "page." Use the large rectangle to cut three "book cover" pieces and one "page" piece. Appliqué the back cover to the background fabric, leaving the left seam allowance flat. Next, appliqué the "page" fabric on top of the back cover, using ⅜"-wide seam allowances so the back cover shows. To create the front cover, sew two pieces of cover fabric, right sides together, leaving the left side open. Turn the cover right side out and press. Lay the front cover over the "page" and baste on the left side. To finish, cover the left seam allowances with the spine of the book. Embellish the front cover with a "book plate," making an embroidered or inked title.

Back cover

"Page" fabric

Front cover

Album

Album Basket

Album Basket
©1991 Mimi Dietrich

Then, add an inscription inside the book. This would be perfect for a wedding or anniversary quilt. Sew a small button to the front cover. Add a loop of thread to the inside back cover to close the book.

6. Embroider the French knots to add baby's breath to your bouquet.

Woven Basket

1. Trace the design onto your background fabric.

2. The basket handle may be appliquéd as a flat ¼" stem, or you can make two ¼"-wide stem pieces and twist them to create a dimensional handle. Cut two ½"-wide bias strips 10" long and baste the raw edges to form ¼"-wide stems. Pin the cut edges inside the placement line of the black-eyed Susan, then twist the two pieces to form the handle, always keeping the seam allowances of the strips next to the background fabric. Pin the handle as you form the twist, then appliqué the edges to the background. Cut the ends to extend ¼" under the tulip.

3. To stitch a woven basket, baste ten ¼"-wide stems cut from basket fabric. Cut the strips ½" longer than the lines in the pattern. Baste the five center vertical strips to the background fabric. Avoid placing basting stitches where the horizontal basket lines cross. Weave the horizontal strips over and under the vertical strips and baste. Appliqué the strips, then add the side vertical strips. Finally, appliqué the basket base and the top edge of the basket.

4. Referring to "Appliqué Methods" (page 7) and "Dimensional Techniques" (page 8), stitch the pieces in the following order:
   - ⅛" stems
   - leaves
   - folded buds
   - gathered bud
   - posy
   - layered rose
   - bluebells

5. Appliqué the tulip in three pieces, beginning with the center petal. Add the two outer petals, stitching them together at the bottom.

6. Appliqué each petal separately on the black-eyed Susan, leaving the seam allowance at the top open. Cover the seam allowances as you add the top of the flower. Embroider a few French knots for a realistic look.

7. Embroider the French knots to add baby's breath to your bouquet.

Woven Basket
©1991 Mimi Dietrich

Flower Vase

1. Trace the design onto your background fabric.
2. Referring to "Appliqué Methods" (page 7) and "Dimensional Techniques" (page 8), stitch the pieces in the following order:
    ⅛" stems
    leaves
    folded buds
3. Appliqué the body and base of the vase, extending the top of the vase under the gathered flowers. Appliqué the vase handles, then add the three circles to finish the vase.
4. Appliqué the gathered flowers (pages 10–11).

Flower Vase

Flower Vase
©1991 Mimi Dietrich

Fruit Bowl

1. Trace the design onto your background fabric.

2. Referring to "Appliqué Methods" (page 7) and "Dimensional Techniques" (page 8), stitch the pieces in the following order:
     ⅛" stems
     leaves
     gathered bud

3. Appliqué the base of the bowl, extending the top seam allowance under the bowl. Appliqué the bowl.

4. The pineapple is a symbol of hospitality. Search for the perfect fabric to create the texture of the pineapple. Appliqué the body of the pineapple, then add the top.

5. Appliqué the posy, center circle, then the grapes. The grapes can be all one color, or shades of purple for a realistic touch.

6. Appliqué the peach, then the top leaves.

7. The pansy is stitched in three pieces. Appliqué the top petals first, overlap the center petals, then add the bottom petals. Add a few straight stitches with embroidery floss to bring the pansy to life.

8. Appliqué each daisy petal separately, leaving the top seam allowance open. A small bit of fiberfill may be stuffed into each petal. Cover the seam allowances as you add the top of the flower. Embroider a few French knots for a realistic look.

9. Appliqué the strawberries, leaving the top of the seam allowance open to lie beneath the cap. Appliqué the strawberry caps, covering the raw edges of the berries. Use the stem stitch to embroider the berry stems.

24

Fruit Bowl

Fruit Bowl
©1991 Mimi Dietrich

Cornucopia

1. Trace the design onto your background fabric.

2. Appliqué the cornucopia, starting with the smallest piece. Appliqué the curve of each piece, letting the seam allowance lie flat under the piece that overlaps it. Continue adding pieces, covering the raw seam allowances.

3. Referring to "Appliqué Methods" (page 7) and "Dimensional Techniques" (page 8), stitch the pieces in the following order:
   - ⅛" stems
   - leaves
   - folded buds
   - gathered bud
   - posy
   - layered rose
   - yoyo flowers

4. To make the circle flower, prepare seven circles. Stitch the six outer circles first. As you stitch the first one, leave a small opening so that the last one can be placed under the first. Finish the flower with the center circle. A bit of fiberfill in the center circle will add dimension.

5. Appliqué the tulips in three pieces, beginning with the center petal. Add the two outer petals, stitching them together at the bottom.

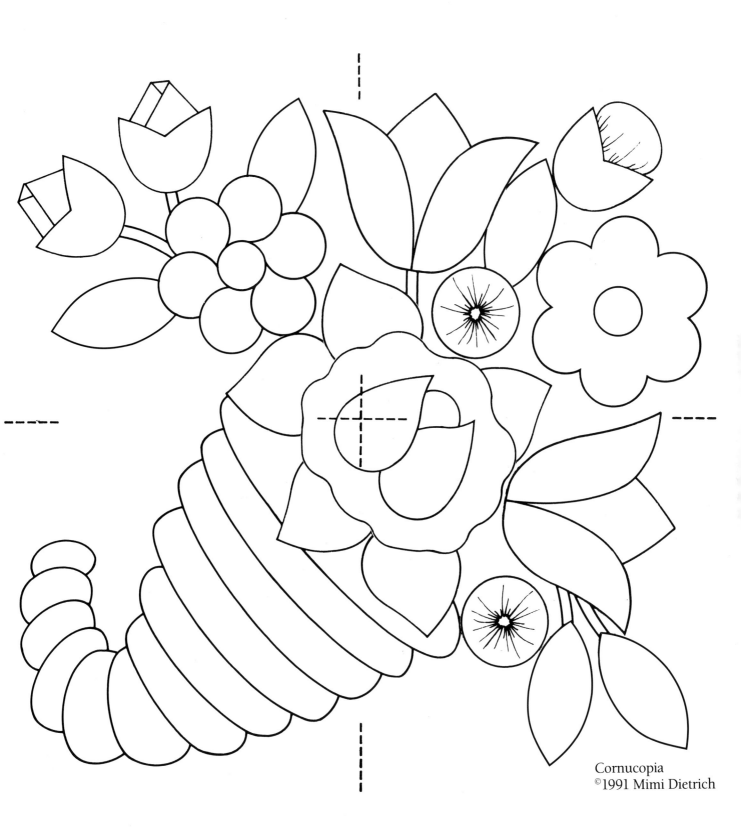

Cornucopia
©1991 Mimi Dietrich

Blossoms 'n' Birds

1. Trace the design onto your background fabric.

2. Referring to "Appliqué Methods" (page 7) and "Dimensional Techniques" (page 8), stitch the pieces in the following order:
    ⅛" stems
    ¼" stems
    leaves
    folded bud
    posy
    gathered flower

3. Appliqué the birds in two separate pieces, first the body, then the wing. Add a French knot or a bead for the birds' eyes. For fun, stuff the wings lightly or line them and keep them unattached. Choose fabrics to simulate the texture of the birds' feathers.

4. Appliqué each daisy petal separately, leaving the top seam allowance open. A small bit of fiberfill may be stuffed into each petal. Cover the seam allowances as you add the top of the flower. Embroider a few French knots for a realistic look.

Blossoms 'n' Birds

Blossoms 'n' Birds
©1991 Mimi Dietrich

29

Heart Wreath

1. Trace the design onto your background fabric.

2. Referring to "Appliqué Methods" (page 7) and "Dimensional Techniques" (page 8), stitch the pieces in the following order:

    ⅛" stems at the bottom of the wreath
    ¼" stems at the top of the wreath
    leaves
    posy
    layered rose
    yoyo flowers (made with 1¾" circles)
    gathered blossoms
    bluebells
    bow

3. Appliqué the tulip in three pieces, beginning with the center petal. Add the two outer petals, stitching them together at the bottom.

4. The pansy is stitched in three pieces. Appliqué the top petals first, overlap the center petals, then add the bottom petals. Add a few straight stitches with embroidery floss to bring the pansy to life.

Heart Wreath

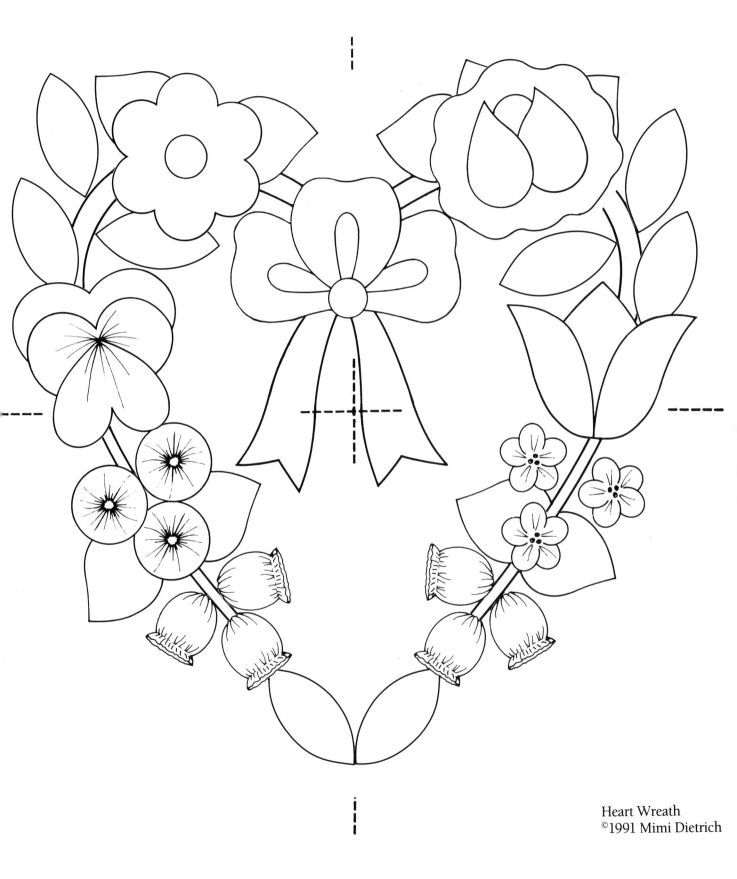

Heart Wreath
©1991 Mimi Dietrich

Posy Wreath

1. Trace the design onto your background fabric.
2. Referring to "Appliqué Methods" (page 7) and "Dimensional Techniques" (page 8), stitch the pieces in the following order:
   ¼" stems
   leaves
   folded buds
   posies
   flower centers (circles)

Posy Wreath

Posy Wreath
©1991 Mimi Dietrich

Love Wreath

1. Trace the design onto your background fabric.

2. Referring to "Appliqué Methods" (page 7) and "Dimensional Techniques" (page 8), stitch the pieces in the following order:

   ¼" stems
   leaves
   folded buds
   gathered flowers
   bow

3. The heart in this wreath adds a touch of love to your quilt. Appliqué the heart at the top of the wreath. Clip the top center of the heart so the seam allowance will turn easily.

Love Wreath

Love Wreath
©1991 Mimi Dietrich

Bird Wreath

1. Trace the design onto your background fabric.

2. Referring to "Appliqué Methods" (page 7) and "Dimensional Techniques" (page 8), stitch the pieces in the following order:
   - ⅛" stems
   - leaves
   - folded buds
   - gathered flower

3. Appliqué the bird in three separate pieces. Appliqué the left wing first, then the body, then the right wing. Add a French knot or a bead for the bird's eye. For fun, stuff the wings lightly or line them and keep them unattached. Choose fabrics to simulate the texture of the bird's feathers.

Bird Wreath

Bird Wreath
©1991 Mimi Dietrich

Bluebell Wreath

1. Trace the design onto your background fabric.
2. Referring to "Appliqué Methods" (page 7) and "Dimensional Techniques" (page 8), stitch the pieces in the following order:
   ¼" stems
   leaves
   bluebells
   bow
3. Add embroidered stems to the bluebells, using the stem stitch.

Bluebell Wreath

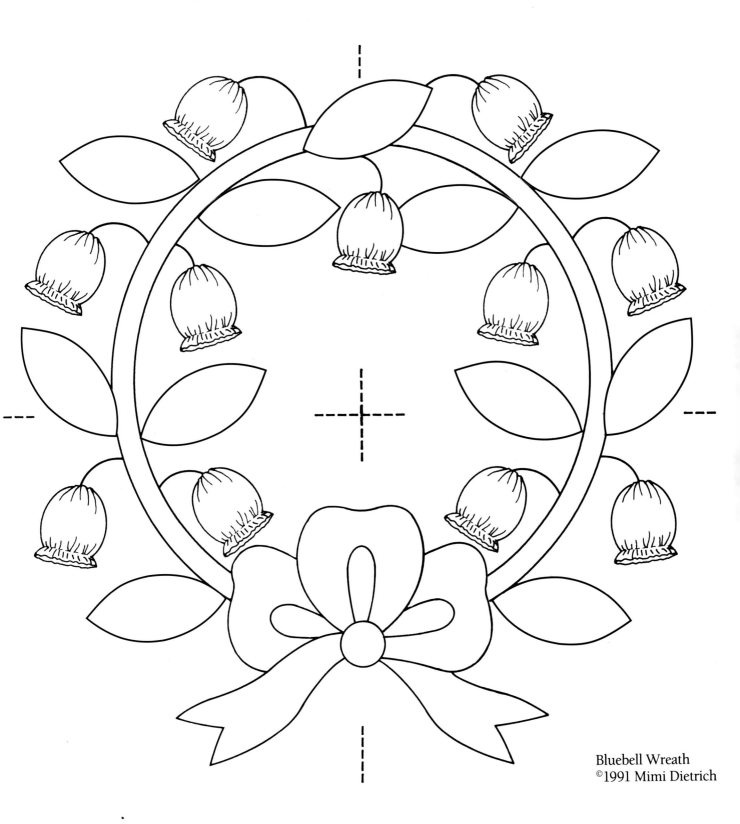

Bluebell Wreath
©1991 Mimi Dietrich

Lyre Wreath

1. Trace the design onto your background fabric.

2. Referring to "Appliqué Methods" (page 7) and "Dimensional Techniques" (page 8), stitch the pieces in the following order:
   - ⅛" stems
   - leaves
   - circles
   - ribbon

3. The lyre symbolizes a love of music. Make its strings by stitching ⅛" stems or thin gold braid to the lyre string lines. The strings should extend ¼" under the lyre at each end. Position the lyre over the stitched strings. Appliqué the inside edge of the lyre first, then the outside edge.

Lyre Wreath

Lyre Wreath
©1991 Mimi Dietrich

Thistle Wreath

1. Trace the design onto your background fabric.
2. Referring to "Appliqué Methods" (page 7) and "Dimensional Techniques" (page 8), stitch the pieces in the following order:
    ¼" stems
    leaves
    ribbon
3. Cut two rectangles for each size of the folded thistles:
    small, 1¼" x 2½"
    medium, 1⅜" x 3"
    large, 1½" x 3½"
4. Turn under and baste a ¼"-wide seam allowance on three sides of each rectangle, leaving one of the long sides flat.
5. Referring to the pattern drawing, fold each rectangle to form a fan-shaped piece (two tucks in the small, three in the medium, four in the large). Baste the folds in place and press the pieces.
6. Pin the thistles in place. Appliqué the sides of the thistle securely. As you appliqué the top edge, stitch only the fabric that lies flat against the background, allowing the folds to remain free.
7. Appliqué the bottoms of the thistles, covering the raw edges and securing the folds.
8. Embroider the stems, using the stem stitch and adding small straight stitches at the tips.

Thistle Wreath

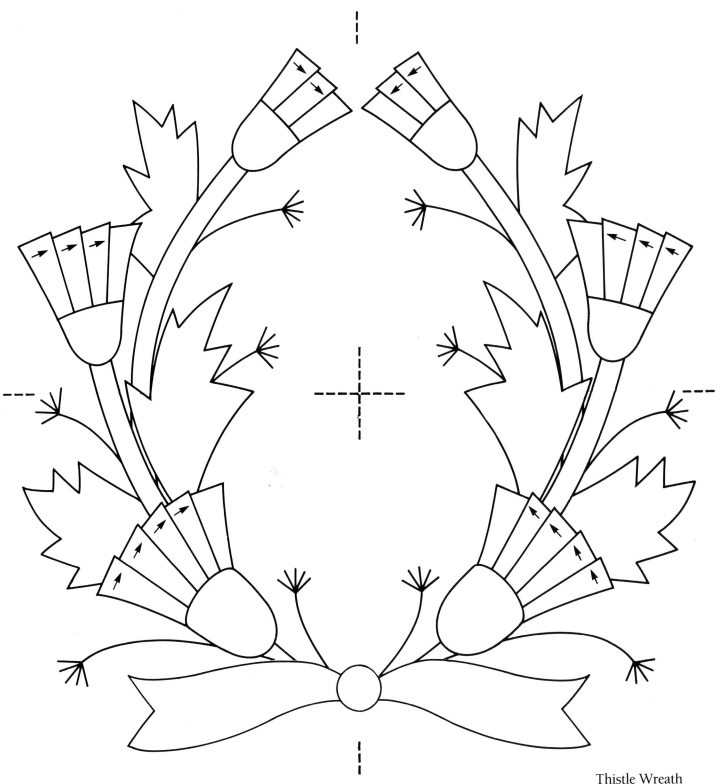

Thistle Wreath
©1991 Mimi Dietrich

Sweet Pea Wreath

1. Trace the design onto your background fabric.
2. Referring to "Appliqué Methods" (page 7) and "Dimensional Techniques" (page 8), appliqué the leaves.
3. Use the stem stitch to embroider the sweet pea vines.
4. Appliqué the sweet pea flowers, using the lettered pieces as a guide. Appliqué piece "a" first, extending the seam allowance under piece "b." Continue adding pieces, covering all raw edges with piece "e."
5. To make the buds, cut a 1¼"-diameter circle from pink fabric. Fold the circle in quarters and gather the raw edges together tightly. Baste the bud to the background fabric. Cover the raw edges as you appliqué the green base over the bud.

Sweet Pea Wreath

Grape Wreath

1. Trace the design onto your background fabric.
2. Referring to "Appliqué Methods" (page 7) and "Dimensional Techniques" (page 8), stitch the pieces in the following order:
    1/8" stems at the top
    1/4" stems at the bottom
    leaves
    circles
3. Using a fine-line permanent pen, trace the vine tendrils onto the background fabric. You may also embroider the tendrils, using the stem stitch.

Grape Wreath

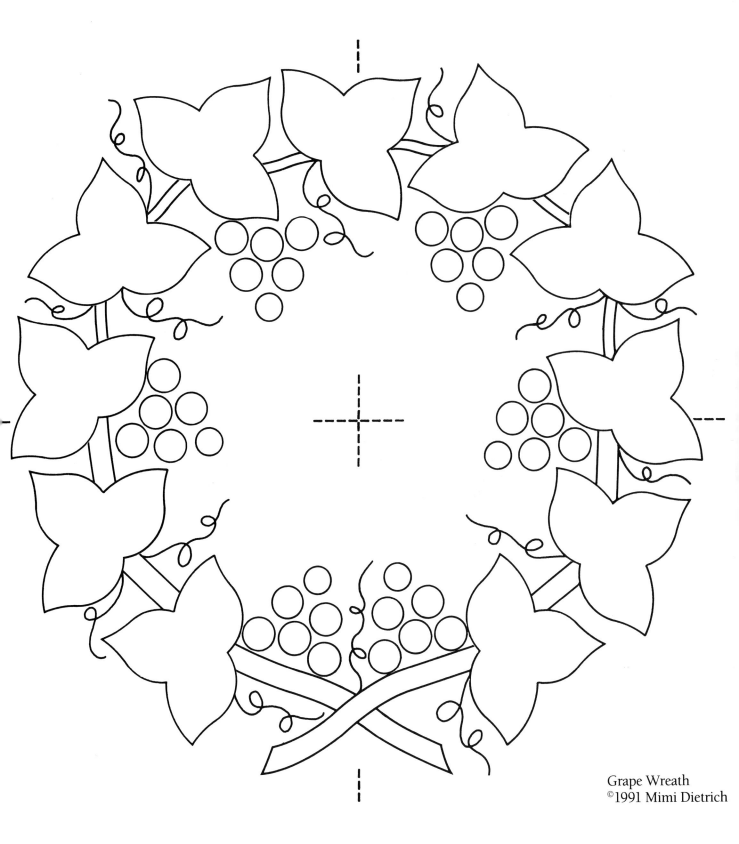

Grape Wreath
©1991 Mimi Dietrich

Strawberry Wreath

1. Trace the design onto your background fabric.
2. Referring to "Appliqué Methods" (page 7) and "Dimensional Techniques" (page 8), stitch the pieces in the following order:
   ¼" stems
   leaves
   gathered blossoms
3. Appliqué the strawberries, leaving the top of the seam allowance open to be covered by the cap. Appliqué the strawberry caps, covering the raw edges of the berries.
4. Use the stem stitch to embroider the berry stems.

Strawberry Wreath

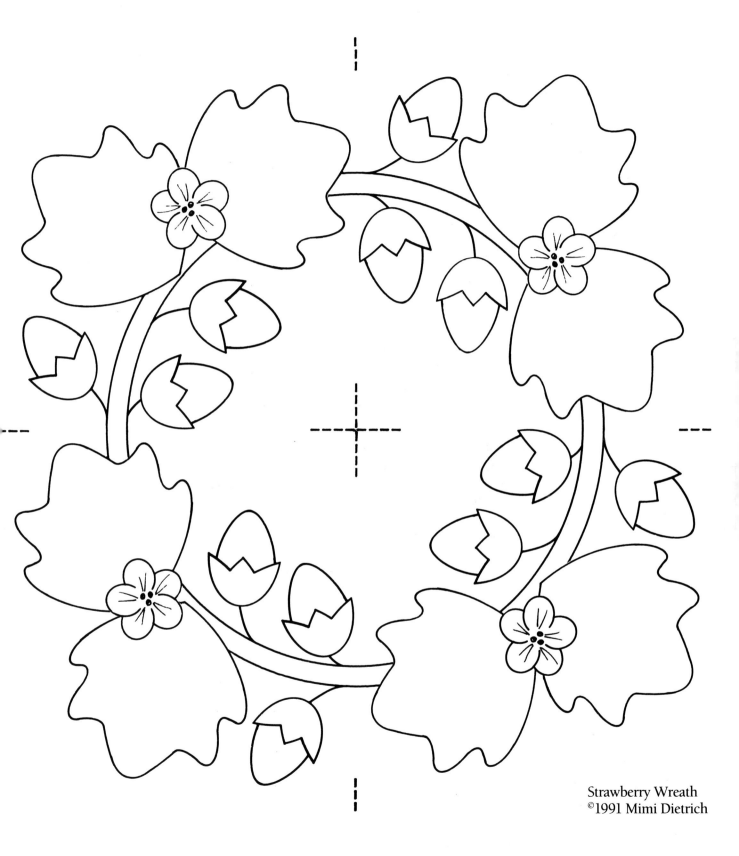

Strawberry Wreath
©1991 Mimi Dietrich

Autumn Wreath

1. Trace the design onto your background fabric.
2. Referring to "Appliqué Methods" (page 7) and "Dimensional Techniques" (page 8), stitch the pieces in the following order:
   ⅛" stems
   leaves
   circles
   ribbon
3. Appliqué the small, round part of the acorns first, leaving the top of the seam allowance open to be covered by the caps. Then appliqué the acorn caps, covering the raw edges of the acorns. For a dimensional effect, line the acorns, keeping them unattached.

Autumn Wreath

51

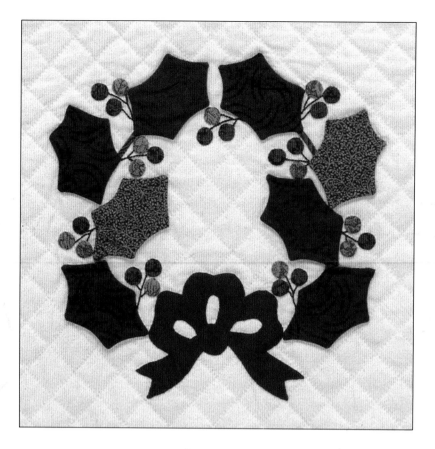

Holly Wreath

1. Trace the design onto your background fabric.
2. Referring to "Appliqué Methods" (page 7) and "Dimensional Techniques" (page 8), stitch the pieces in the following order:
    - ⅛" stems
    - leaves
    - circles
    - bow
3. Embroider the berry stems, using the stem stitch.

Holly Wreath

Holly Wreath
©1991 Mimi Dietrich

Borders

How to Use the Border Patterns

The four border patterns in this book are planned so that any border design can be used with any arrangement of blocks. The 10" repeated border patterns are compatible with the 10" finished block size. The border corner patterns include a ¼"-wide allowance for the narrow inner border.

To make a full-size border pattern for your quilt, choose one design and trace the 10" border pattern. For a four-block quilt, trace the border twice; for a nine-block quilt, trace the border three times to correspond with the number of blocks next to the border. Also trace the corner pattern twice. Tape the traced patterns together to form a complete border.

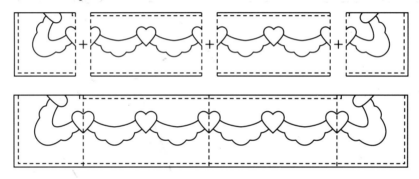

Cut four borders for your quilt from the background fabric. The borders should be cut 5½" wide and 4" longer than the finished size of your quilt.

To mark the appliqué design onto the background border fabric, tape the full-size pattern to a flat surface. Place the border fabric over the pattern, matching the top and bottom edges and extending the extra border fabric equally at each end. Trace the design onto the fabric, using a washable fabric marker.

At this point, I do not trace the corner design onto the fabric border. The four borders should be appliquéd separately before attaching them to your quilt. The corner bow or swag cannot be appliquéd until the border is mitered. I like to wait until the quilt is completely constructed, then trace the corner design and finish the appliquéd border.

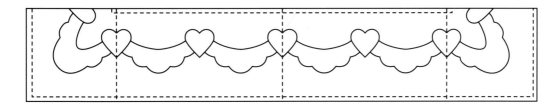

Swags and Hearts

Traditional swags, connected by hearts, create a lovely frame for a quilt. Choose a multicolored floral print for the swags, then use colors from the swag fabric to stitch the designs. Appliqué the swags first, then the hearts.

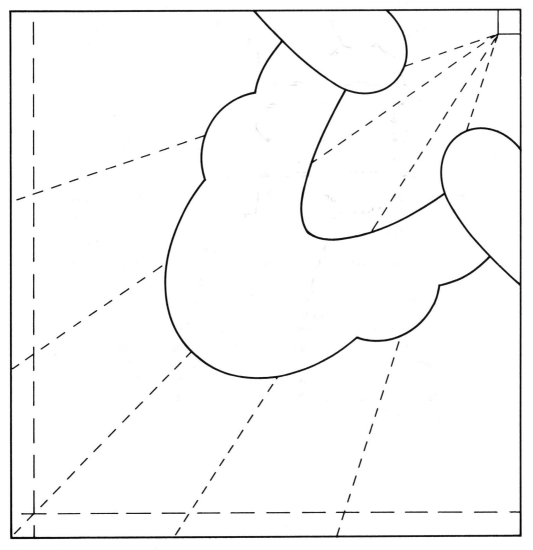

Corner Pattern

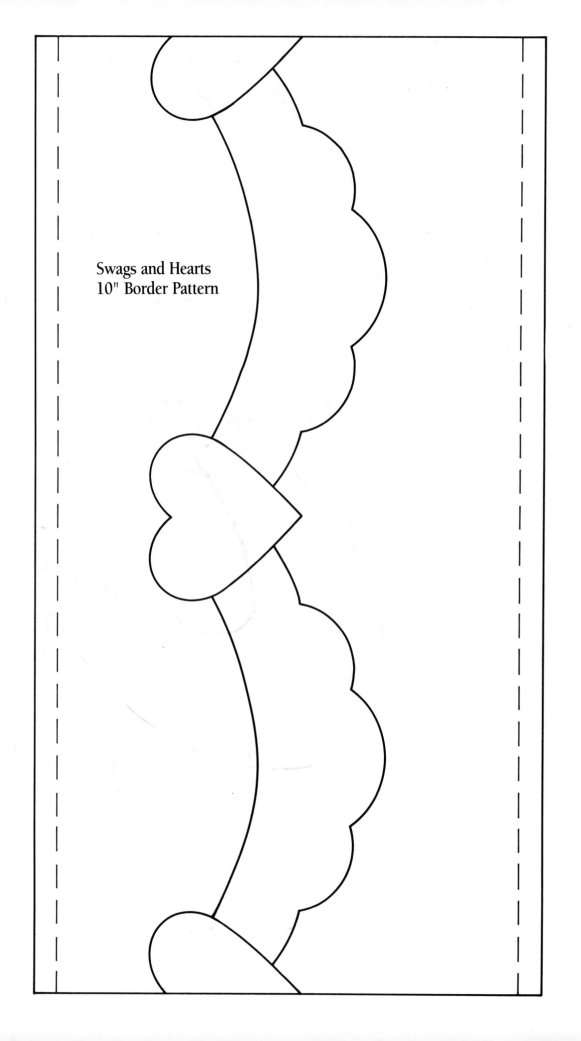

Swags and Hearts
10" Border Pattern

Swags and Tassels

Dimension is added to this traditional border with tassels created from yoyo flowers and bluebells. Appliqué the swags first, then the stems, yoyo flowers, and bluebells.

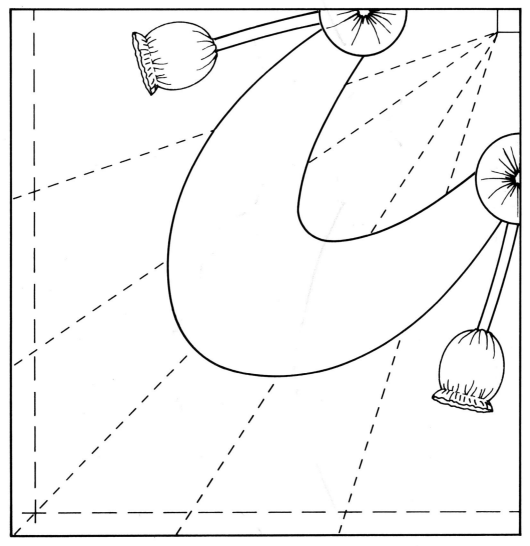

Corner Pattern

57

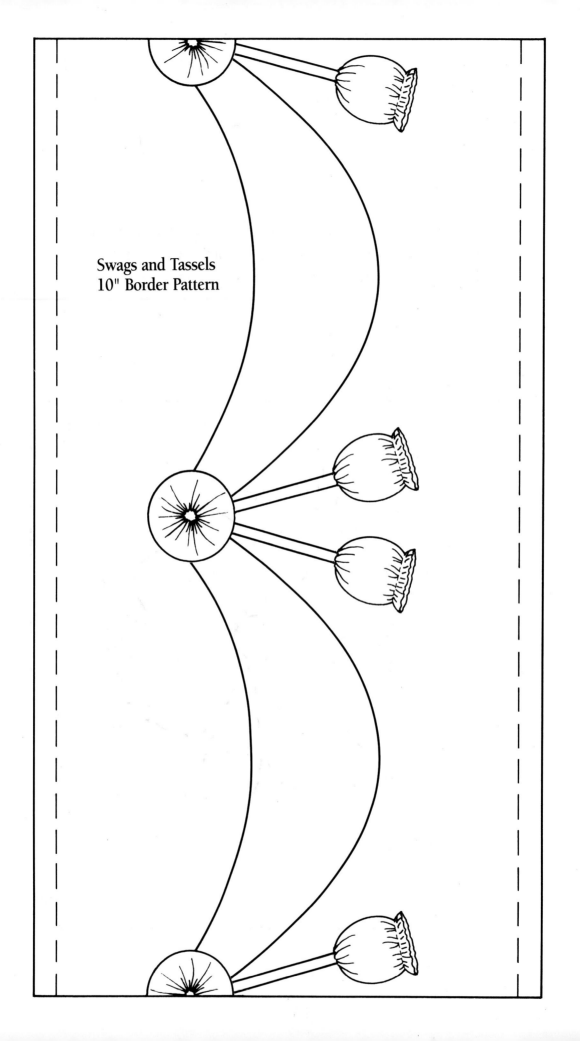

Swags and Tassels
10" Border Pattern

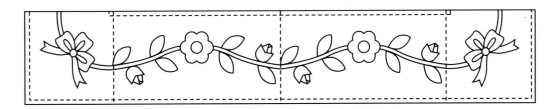

Ribbons and Vines

Vines of folded buds and posies are tied together with bows in the corners. Appliqué the ¼"-wide stems first, then the leaves, folded buds, and posies. Add the bows after the quilt has been constructed.

Corner Pattern

Ribbons and Vines
10" Border Pattern

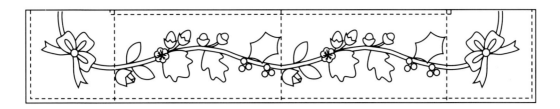

Four Seasons

The Four Seasons border repeats elements from the Four Seasons block designs. Appliqué the ¼"-wide stems first, then the leaves, buds, berries, and acorns. Add the bows after the quilt has been constructed.

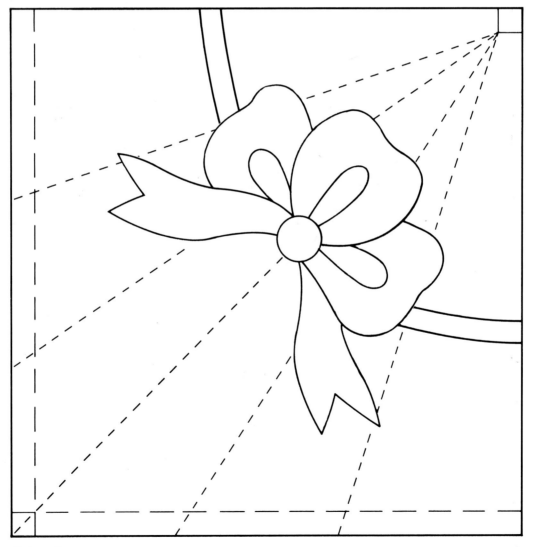

Corner Pattern

Four Seasons
10" Border Pattern

Gallery

Traditional Album, appliquéd by students of Mimi Dietrich, 1991, Baltimore, Maryland, quilted by Mimi Dietrich, 41" x 41". Traditional Baltimore Album colors create a rich effect on a printed muslin background.

Detail showing the inscription written inside the open album

Bouquets and Baskets, appliquéd by the Catonsville Quilt and Tea Society, 1991, Baltimore, Maryland, quilted by Joan Weiss, 31" x 31". Soft pastels chosen from the border fabric bring the flowers in the baskets and bouquets to life. A special inscription written or embroidered in the album would make a perfect wedding or anniversary quilt.

American Beauty Antique, appliquéd by students of Mimi Dietrich, 1991, Baltimore, Maryland, quilted by Linda Daigle, 31" x 31". Shaded hand-dyed fabrics on a tea-dyed background give an antique look to this delightful quilt.

Four Seasons, appliquéd by students of Mimi Dietrich, 1991, Baltimore, Maryland, quilted by Barbara Johnson, 31" x 31". Reds, greens, and golds bring the four seasons to life. The border design repeats the elements in the appliquéd blocks.

Blue Bouquets, appliquéd by students of Mimi Dietrich, 1991, Baltimore, Maryland, quilted by Joan Glynn Wille, 31" x 31". Blue fabrics selected from a quilt made by Violet Hopkins create a monochromatic design reminiscent of blue china designs.

Springtime in Baltimore, appliquéd by students of Mimi Dietrich, 1991, Baltimore, Maryland, quilted by Leigh Zimmerman, 41" x 41". A palette of pastels gives a soft look to this quilt. During the class, many students stitched yellow ribbons into their album quilts as they watched the Gulf War on television. Yellow ribbons were added to the border of this quilt to remember friends and family who served our country.

Victorian Album, appliquéd by students of Mimi Dietrich, 1991, Baltimore, Maryland, quilted by Mim Levenson, 31" x 31". Using her wonderful leftover pieces, Pat Mueller chose a palette of pinks and purples from the border print to create an album quilt using her favorite colors.

Black Beauty, appliquéd by students of Mimi Dietrich, 1991, Baltimore, Maryland, quilted by Margaret Ward, 31" x 31". Borders cut from a floral-striped fabric create a dramatic frame for appliqués stitched on a black background.

Create Your Own Designs

Create your own bouquet arrangements; use your favorite techniques! Many of the elements in these designs are similar in size and can be easily substituted for one another. Simply trace the part of the design that you like, omitting the part you wish to replace. Then, place the tracing paper over the desired flower, trace, and enjoy your new creation!

Some elements that substitute easily are:

folded buds - gathered buds

layered roses - gathered flowers

tulips - black-eyed Susans

posies - roses - tulips - pansies

bluebells - gathered blossoms - yoyo flowers

Flower shapes cut from a floral print can be substituted for any similarly sized flower.

Instead of the round circle in the center of the posies, use a little gathered blossom.

Substitute a cluster of little gathered blossoms for a larger flower. Create a small bouquet of violets or forget-me-nots, using purple or blue fabrics.

Add variety to your designs by trying several different techniques for partial leaves within the same block, such as flat leaves, pinched leaves, and lined leaves.

Use the "Lined Leaves" technique (page 9) for other shapes, including acorns, strawberries, bow streamers, bird wings, and the tulip center.

Many of the flower patterns and techniques can be used in other appliqué designs. Simply substitute designs in this book for appliqué designs with similar shapes and sizes. If a design is not the exact size, use a photocopy machine to enlarge or reduce the flower size.

The four borders in this book are planned so that any border design can be used with any arrangement of blocks. The 10" repeated design is compatible with the 10" finished block size. Also, elements in the borders can be redesigned. The plain curved swags can be exchanged for the scalloped swags; the tassels can be exchanged for the hearts. If you like, use a posy or layered rose from your quilt in place of the hearts or tassels.

Choose your favorites and create a special quilt all your own!

folded buds - gathered buds

posies - roses - tulips - pansies

layered roses - gathered flowers

tulips - black-eyed Susans

bluebells - gathered blossoms - yoyo flowers

Finishing

Quilt Construction

If you have cut your appliqué blocks larger than 10½" square, you need to trim the blocks to an even 10½" square. To do this easily, cut a sheet of template plastic exactly 10½" square. Mark the vertical and horizontal center lines on the plastic. Refer to the pattern to help you center the template on your stitched design. Use a washable fabric marker to draw around the edges of the template plastic, then cut with scissors or a rotary cutter.

Place the blocks on a table in the desired layout.

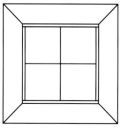

Four Block Construction

If you are using four blocks, sew the top two blocks together, using ¼"-wide seam allowances, then sew the bottom two blocks together. Press the seam allowances open. Sew the top and bottom rows together, carefully matching the center seams. Press the seams open.

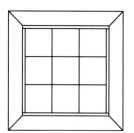

Nine Block Construction

If you are using nine blocks, sew the top row together, using ¼"-wide seam allowances, then the second row, then the third. Press the seams open. Sew the top two rows together, then add the bottom row. Press the seams open.

Note: I find that pressing the seams open on light-background appliqué blocks distributes the "shadow" of the seam allowances equally on either side of the seam. This also distributes the thickness of the seam allowance for quilting.

To add the small borders, cut four strips of border fabric ⅞" wide. A four-block quilt requires two strips 20½" long and two strips 21¾" long. A nine-block quilt requires two strips 30½" long and two strips 31¾" long.

Using ¼"-wide seam allowances, sew the shorter strips to the sides of the quilt. Press the seams toward the border strips. Sew the longer strips to the top and bottom of the quilt. Press the seams toward the border strips.

The outer borders are cut 5½" wide and should be cut 4" longer than the finished size of the quilt. Fold the borders to find the center of the appliqué design, then match the center of the border to the center of the quilt edge. Sew the borders to the edges of the quilt, leaving ¼" unstitched at the beginning and end of the seams. Press the seams toward the narrow borders. Pressing this way pads the narrow border and prevents the seams from shadowing through the light background fabric.

To miter a corner, match the border strips, right sides together, folding the quilt corner diagonally. Use a long ruler to extend the line of the diagonal fold into the border. Mark the line to extend from the end of the border seam out to the edge of the quilt. Many rulers are marked with a 45° angle to check the line placement. Sew along the marked line. Check to make sure the border lies flat, then cut away the extra fabric, leaving a ¼"-wide seam allowance. Press the seam open.

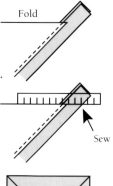

Quilting

Quilting stitches outline and define your appliqué pieces, create a design in the background area, and add a wonderful texture to your quilt. Quilting stitches are short running stitches used to hold the top, batting, and backing of your quilt together. For hand quilting, a light or low-loft polyester batting will provide a traditional look while helping your needle glide easily through the layers.

Traditionally, appliquéd quilts are stitched with two kinds of quilting. The first outlines the appliqué pieces. The stitches are placed just outside the appliqué, adding dimension and clarity to the appliqué pieces. The stitches go through the background of the quilt, batting, and backing, just outside the appliqué edges. Many appliqué pieces will appear to be stuffed after this quilting is completed. Sometimes, quilting stitches are used to outline details within the design, such as rose petals. In this case, the quilting stitches go through the appliqués as well as the other layers of the quilt.

The second kind of quilting is background quilting. Straight lines or designs are stitched through the background fabric, batting, and backing. Background quilting does not usually continue through the appliqués.

After the quilt top has been constructed, mark the quilting design onto the background fabric. A diagonal grid is traditionally used to mark appliqué backgrounds.

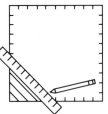

To mark the background quilting design, place dots at 1" intervals along the edges of the 10" blocks. Use a long ruler to connect the dots and mark the diagonal lines. Lines on adjacent blocks will connect for an overall design. Use a fabric marking pencil that will wash out after the quilt is completed. Test the marker on a scrap of background fabric before marking your quilt.

The diagonal lines may be quilted in one direction, or in both directions for a lattice grid. In a four-block quilt, you can quilt the diagonals so they originate in the center of the quilt.

Mark the border quilting lines 1" apart. To help keep the lines straight, place dots at 1" intervals along the outside edge of the narrow border and also on the raw edge of the quilt. Start your markings in the border center, then connect the dots for evenly spaced lines. In the corners, refer to the pattern for quilting lines.

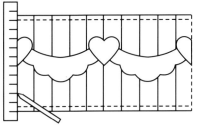

Before you start to quilt, baste together the top, batting, and backing of the quilt. This secures the three layers and keeps the fabric from slipping. Starting in the center, baste parallel lines. The basting lines should be 4"–6"

apart. The more rows of basting you have, the better the layers will stay together. Carefully baste around the edges to keep the quilt top from stretching.

To begin quilting, tie a single knot in the end of an 18" length of quilting thread. Insert the needle through the top layer of the quilt, about ¾" away from the point where you want to start stitching. Slide the needle through the batting layer and bring the needle out at the starting point. Gently tug on the thread until the knot pops through the fabric and is buried in the batting. 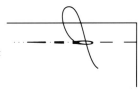 Begin quilting, making a small running stitch that goes through all layers. Take two, three, or four stitches at a time, trying to keep them straight and even.

To end quilting stitches, make a single knot in the thread about ¼" from your quilt top. Take one more stitch into the quilt, tugging the knot into the batting layer and bringing the needle out ¾" away from the stitches. Clip the thread and let the end disappear into your quilt.

This Sequence is Recommended for Quilting:

1. *Quilt around the outside edges of all appliqué pieces in the blocks. This outline quilting will accent your designs and make your appliqué puff slightly.*

2. *Quilt along the inner and outer edges of the narrow border. Be careful to keep this line straight so the quilt does not become distorted.*

3. *Quilt the background design of the quilt. The diagonal lines will ease as you stitch the bias of the fabric.*

4. *Outline quilt the border appliqué designs.*

5. *Quilt the background design in the border area.*

Binding

Binding adds the finishing touch to your quilt. The bindings of Baltimore Bouquet quilts repeat the fabric used as the narrow accent border in the quilt. Complete all of the quilting before applying the binding.

1. Baste around the edge of your quilt to securely hold the three layers together. Trim any excess threads, batting, or backing even with the front of the quilt.

2. Cut four 2"-wide strips of binding fabric across the 44" width of fabric. These can be cut quickly with a rotary cutter and a clear, acrylic ruler.

3. Sew the four strips together, using diagonal seams, to create one long strip of binding. To make diagonal seams the easy way, cross two strip ends at right angles, right sides together. Lay these on a flat surface and imagine the strips as a large letter "A." Draw a line across the crossed pieces to "cross the A," then sew along the line. Your seam will be exact, and you can unfold a continuous strip.

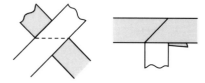

Trim off the excess fabric, leaving a ¼"-wide seam allowance.

Press this seam open to distribute the thickness of the seam.

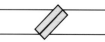

4. Fold the binding strip in half lengthwise, wrong sides together, and press with a hot steam iron.

5. Match the two cut edges of the binding strip to the front cut edge of the quilt. Start sewing the strip approximately 6" from one of the corners, using a ¼"-wide seam. For durability, sew this seam by machine.

6. To miter the corners of the binding, stop stitching ¼" from the corner and backtack.

Fold the binding diagonally as shown, so that it extends straight up from the second edge of the quilt.

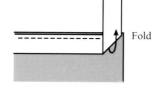

Then, fold the binding down even with the second edge of the quilt. The fold should be even with the first edge. Start sewing the binding ¼" from the fold, making sure to backtack.

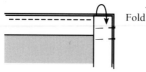

As you fold the corner to the back of the quilt, a folded miter will appear on the front.

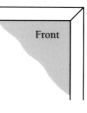

On the back, fold one side first, then the other, to create a miter on the back.

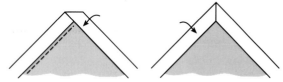

7. To connect the ends of the binding, allow the end to overlap the beginning edge by 2". Cut the end diagonally, with the shortest end of the diagonal on top, nearest to you. Turn the diagonal edge under ¼" and insert the beginning "tail" inside the diagonal fold.

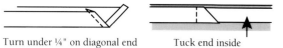

Turn under ¼" on diagonal end   Tuck end inside

Continue sewing the binding onto the quilt. When you turn this area to the back of the quilt, hand stitch the diagonal fold.

8. Fold the binding over the edge of the quilt. The folded edge of the binding should cover the stitching on the back of the quilt. Hand stitch the binding to the back of the quilt, using the traditional appliqué stitch.

70

*Many thanks to the following friends and students, who made color decisions,
appliquéd, sewed, basted, quilted, and made Baltimore Bouquets come alive!*

Sharon Adams	Diana Harper	Barbara Rasch
Barbara Alexander	Phyllis Hess	Marie Rock
Barbara Austin	Susan Hodges	Carol Rogers
Sharon Baker	Violet Hopkins	Libbie Rollman
Katharyn Black	Lynn Irwin	Christine Russell
Gertrude Braan	Barbara Johnson	Vivian Schafer
Barbara Brown	Charlie Jones	Laurie Scott
Sue Brunt	Corinne Kerns	Linda Simms
Norma Campbell	Kathleen Laffey	Bonnie Strickroth
Ann Christy	Mim Levenson	Fran Timmins
Karen Cohn	Debbie Machiran	Phyllis Van Meerhaeghe
Anne Connery	Judy Madel	V. Jeanne Vaughn
Ruby Costea	Barbara Ellis McMahon	Marsha Dowler Vogel
Joan Costello	Billie J. Meseke	Barbara Wagner
Linda Daigle	Chris Miller	Paige Walbert
Estelle Davis	Pat Mueller	Margaret Ward
Eleanor Eckman	Patti Muller	Carol Neitzel Watson
Eileen Finnegan	Marilyn Novak	Joan Weiss
Lillias Fradl	Marian Nozinski	Lois Wehren
Sherry Fulkoski	Barbara O'Brien	Jackie Wilcox
Kass Green	Elsie Page	Joan Glynn Wille
Charity Harbison	Mary Parent	Rosemarie Wittig
Julianne Hardy	Sandy Pfau	Sally Zeller
Jean Harmon	Carolyn Piper	Leigh Zimmerman